This book belongs to:

_____

This book contributes to your child's early understanding of the reading process.

As you read together, practise saying the letter sounds. Remember that the letter name is **A**, as in ABC and the sound is **a** as in apple.

Help your child to trace the letter with his finger and to write it in the air. Singing the alphabet and the letter names is a great way to remember the sequence. Making letter shapes using play dough will help, too.

A catalogue record for this book is available from the British Library

Published by Ladybird Books Ltd
80 Strand, London, WC2R 0RL
A Penguin Company

016-18 17 16
© LADYBIRD BOOKS LTD MMVIII
LADYBIRD and the device of a Ladybird are trademarks of Ladybird Books Ltd

ISBN: 978-1-84646-813-1

Printed in China

abc

illustrated by Mark Airs

a

apple

b

butterfly

C

car

d

dinosaur

e

elephant

f

feather

g

gorilla

h

helicopter

i

igloo

j

jigsaw

k

kangaroo

l

lamb

m

monkey

n

1 2 3

numbers

O

octopus

p

pencil

q

queen

r

robot

S

strawberry

t

tortoise

u

umbrella

van

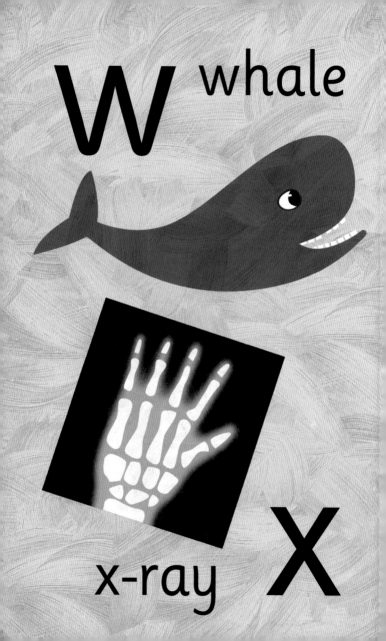

W whale

x-ray X

y yacht

zebra z